Infant Ba̴
Common Worship

Colin Buchanan
Bishop of Woolwich

GROVE BOOKS LIMITED
RIDLEY HALL RD CAMBRIDGE CB3 9HU

Contents

Acknowledgments

I have written a fair amount on infant baptism in my time (some of which is mentioned in footnotes further on), but the new *Common Worship* books in the Church of England from late 2000 have triggered here another, in line with the range of other Grove booklets relating to the new texts. I was in the past deeply involved in the creation of the previous baptismal texts of the Church of England, and that emerges below. But for the *Common Worship* texts I was on the General Synod Revision Committee on Initiation Services which sat for nearly two years, and so have stood close to these texts also. The Group for the Renewal of Worship (GROW) which I chair gave me opportunity to air much of the contents of this booklet at our Swanwick Conference 'Common Worship and Beyond' in January 2001; and thanks are due to the two members of the Group who have assisted me by reading this booklet in draft, and commenting helpfully on it, that is, Mark Earey and Christopher Byworth. In line with the Group's normal procedures, for better or worse I take responsibility for the ultimate product.

The Cover Illustration is by Peter Ashton

First Impression April 2001
ISSN 0144-1728
ISBN 1 85174 460 6

1
Introduction

Infant baptism has been a matter on which I have been writing for over thirty years, a concern traceable back as a serious theological subject in my own life to public debates with David Pawson, debates conducted at Tyndale House, Cambridge, once each decade in the mid-1960s, mid-1970s, and late 1980s. These debates also found some written form in the early Grove Booklets on Ministry and Worship, my own, *A Case for Infant Baptism* (No 20, 1973), and the response of David Pawson and my counter-response, *Infant Baptism under Cross-Examination* (No 24, 1974). Both these booklets have remained in print for 27 years at the time of writing, and apparently are still relevant to the needs in the Church of England. It is not, however, sufficient to defend the principle of baptizing infants, if either the liturgy used or the pastoral practice commended severs the perch on which the principle is located. I have therefore in the past written on the rites of infant baptism, not only to draw out their meaning and assist their use, but also to demonstrate that they are in harmony with the kind of justification of infant baptism which is warranted by Scripture.[1]

The main text to which this commentary relates is available by derivation from the section 'Holy Baptism' in the main *Common Worship* Sunday book. It is set out in the folding card which can be purchased from Church House Publishing. It varies very slightly from the text originally authorized from Easter 1998 in *Common Worship: Initiation Services*, as some modifications were provided by Synod in February 2000, when final approval was being given to the rites going into the new book.

Because of the inexplicable decision of the Liturgical Publishing Group not to allow section numbers in *Common Worship* texts, I have occasionally had to use clumsy ways of reference to the official text, but I hope all is clear.

---

1   Following the booklets mentioned above, I wrote no 65, *Liturgy for Initiation* (1979), about the texts authorized for the *ASB* in 1980, and a fullish, more popular, treatment specifically about the *ASB* text in *Anglican Worship Today* (Collins, 1980). In 1986 came no 98, *Policies for Infant Baptism*, replacing my long-since-gone no 3, *Baptismal Discipline* (1972) (but itself now out of print). In 1992 I wrote *Infant Baptism in the Church of England* (Grove Books Ltd—not in this series) to expound the legal situation, with the Canons (see page 24 below) and the *ASB* text on left-hand pages facing a commentary on the right-hand pages. A larger work was my *Infant Baptism and the Gospel* (DLT, 1993), also now out of print. Then, when *Common Worship* texts were authorized, I wrote jointly with Michael Vasey no 145 in this series, *New Initiation Rites: A Commentary on the Services Authorized from Easter 1998* (January 1998). I also offer a popular handling of the issues in M Earey and G Myers (eds), *Common Worship Today* (HarperCollins, 2001); and there is useful scholarship in the chapter by Simon Jones and Phillip Tovey in Paul Bradshaw (ed), *Companion to Common Worship* (SPCK, 2001) and much practical wisdom in Gilly Myers' own Praxis book in the 'Using *Common Worship*' series, *Initiation: A Practical Guide to the New Services* (Praxis/CHP, 2000).

2
The Basis for Baptizing Infants

In terms of the world Churches, to baptize infants, far from being an obvious practice, is actually a highly divisive and misleading one. If, as is claimed, the Pentecostalist strand of evangelical Christianity has numbers now in excess of 400 million (ranking second only to the Roman Catholics), then these, plus the Baptists, Disciples of Christ, Independent Evangelical Churches, and many smaller anti-pedobaptist denominations, provide a great phalanx of opponents of infant baptism. So we cannot affirm in the face of this phalanx that we simply continue infant baptism because it is a received tradition, or, say, an evangelistic opportunity. There has to be a better rationale, or we should discontinue it. And we ourselves, who claim that the Bible is our supreme authority, can hardly live with a good conscience alongside that claim if, in our heart of hearts, we know that infant baptism is actually unbiblical and misleading. We cannot stay here on bad arguments, but merely note the folly of resting on unsure grounds.[2]

My procedure is first to examine the actual evidence of the background to baptism in the Old Testament and of the use of baptism (and related rites or beliefs) in the New Testament; and then to attempt to draw them together into a harmonized doctrinal position which is fair to the teaching of the whole Bible, and particularly the teaching about the gospel, conversion, the church, and the family. I have done this elsewhere at greater length, and refer anyone dissatisfied with the compressed argument here to those places.[3]

Clearly in the New Testament baptism was given to adult converts as part of imparting the gospel to them and of registering their response. Was it

---

2   I note here as counter-productive the following apologias: (i) Any doctrine that infant baptism wipes out the taint of original sin automatically—it seems the Reformers abandoned the teaching that for an infant to die unbaptized is to die outside of God's grace and under his wrath, and that is ferried through in Note 2 of Emergency Baptism in *Pastoral Services* page 198. It must be acknowledged as a pastorally disastrous (yet haunting) construct stemming from too tight a logic by Augustine of Hippo, who turned an existing practice of infant baptism into an absolute necessity in order to cleanse the taint of original sin. (ii) Any doctrine simply that 'Jesus loves the little children.' The gospel passage, Mark 10.13–16, used by Cranmer in 1552, and continued in 1662, went strongly in this direction. It is too frail a foundation for the weight of infant baptism that the liturgical homily in 1552 and 1662 placed upon it, and so virtually played into the hands of opponents. Baptists do know this text! The passage was moved to the Thanksgiving Service in the ASB (pp 215, 220) and in *Common Worship* is among the set passages at the Thanksgiving for the Gift of a Child (see *Pastoral Services*, p 207). It has thus not only no place in an apologia for infant baptism, but is carefully located in relation to a different kind of all-inclusive rite.

3   Primarily in *A Case for Infant Baptism* (1973, No 20 in this series, still in print). David Pawson, wrote a Baptist reply, and I replied again in defence of *A Case*—and his reply and my defence became *Infant Baptism under Cross-Examination* (No 24, 1974, also still in print). A chapter in my bigger book, *Infant Baptism and the Gospel* (DLT, 1993, now out of print), covered the same ground, including a brief discussion of the 'covenantal' principle.

then given to infants? The earliest actual 'camera-shot' evidence that infants were baptized is admittedly not in the New Testament, but in the writings of Tertullian in North Africa around 190–200 AD, where he is trying to change what was then current practice by urging that infants should *not* be baptized.[4] So the practice existed in the second century—when did it begin? Was it there from the start, perfectly traceable in Scripture itself? The following lines of evidence, when put together, point to the answer 'yes.'

1. The Old Testament sign of the covenant of God, circumcision, was given to infants—yet its meaning, according to Paul, was that of a sign of the righteousness which comes through faith (Rom 4.12). Yet baptism is also— indeed far more so—a sign of the righteousness which comes through faith (*cf* Rom 6.3–4, Gal 3.26–27 etc).[5] If circumcision could properly belong to infants before they professed faith, is there not a strong possibility that baptism is also open in appropriate cases to infants?[6]

2. The baptism of proselytes (converts to Judaism) is known in the late first century AD, and families so baptized brought their children into baptism with them.[7] Certainly, in the atmosphere of Roman Empire women could become Jews in their own persons, which may have suggested the need of a ritual initiation other than circumcision. If the practice began round

---

4 His evidence, if marginally surprising to anyone previously unaware of it, is relevant. Firstly, it testifies that infants were being baptized in his time as the received practice of the church. Secondly, he fails to use the knock-down argument—the argument he really needed—that infant baptism had not been practised by the apostles or in the apostolic church (and I suggest that the argument was not available to him, because it *was* an apostolic practice). And thirdly, his opposition is based on the supposed risk godparents take when they 'go bail' for infants without knowing how the youngsters will turn out later (and *that* feature of infant baptism in Tertullian's time does sound like a late second-century growth).

5 There is great importance in the replacement of the old initiatory sign by the new (and we know it *was* replacement, through the battles of Paul to ensure that Gentile converts did not need to be circumcised, whereas all believers in Jesus as Lord, Jew or Gentile, were baptized). The easy juxtaposition of circumcision with baptism in Col 2.10–11 points in the same direction. We can but speculate as to why God changed the sign, but two separate issues are well met by the change— firstly, that Jews of the old covenant needed a further confronting prophetic sign for inclusion in the new; and secondly, that in the new covenant women should be included in their own persons, and not simply by being attached to circumcised males.

6 Ah, but my Baptists friends will say that Old Testament circumcision betokened an automatic inheritance within ethnic Judaism, a belonging to the land and to the people of God which came to all by physical birth. In the New Testament, they go on, new birth is not 'by the will of the flesh or physical descent' and 'God has no grandchildren.' I reply that in the two generations from Abraham to Jacob, which provide the archetypal evidence in relation to circumcision, the two sons of Abraham and then the two sons of Isaac are treated identically *as though* the promise of God's grace pertained in the same way to each of them, but in fact we, with the text of Genesis before us, know that in each generation only one was the true inheritor. So it looks as though the sign of the righteousness which comes through faith was given on the basis of birth in the believing household, though without that automatic earthly inheritance built in which has been used by Baptists to disqualify the evidence from circumcision.

7 Proselytes are mentioned four times in the New Testament, but modern translations vary as to how they render the word (see Matt 23.15; Acts 2.10; 6.5; 13.43). The discussion of the issue of proselyte baptism, including the dating of the evidence, is in J Jeremias, *Infant Baptism in the First Four Centuries* (ET, SCM, 1960) pp 24–40.

the Empire before the 20s AD, then it is a clear background factor in the New Testament.[8] It would add to the likelihood that converts to Christ took their children into Christian baptism with them. There were proselytes present on the Day of Pentecost (Acts 2.10), and they heard that the heart of their existing Judaism was in fact Jesus Christ, that the promise was to them *and to their children*, and that they were now to be baptized into the name of Christ (Acts 2.38–39). If their children had been baptized into Judaism with them, it is almost unimaginable that they did not now take their children into Christian baptism with them.

3. There are the New Testament references to 'households' being baptized: Lydia's (Acts 16.15); the Philippian jailer's (Acts 16.33), Stephanas' (1 Cor 1.16)—and possibly also Crispus' (Acts 18.8). These do not quite say that infants were present among those being baptized (in other words, we still lack 'camera-shot' evidence), but the broad inclusive word for a whole household neither distinguishes the ages of those baptized, nor suggests that all were above a certain age, nor rules out any group as being part of the 'household.' These unselfconscious, passing mentions of New Testament practice are almost of themselves determinative.[9]

4. We need to look at the baptism of adult converts in the New Testament also. They were baptized *on the spot*; indeed it is almost appropriate to say they were *converted in the water*—in principle they entered it as applicants, they emerged from it as converts (see, *eg*, Acts 2.38–41, Acts 8.35–38). So there was no probationary period leading from first profession of faith to later baptism, such as has been usual in most parts of Christian history and missionary practice since. Of course, there have been good pastoral reasons for the introduction of probationary or 'catechumenal' preparation, and there may be good pastoral reasons for thorough preparation for adult baptism today. But the archetypes in the New Testament show no such preparation, and our theologizing about baptism must work from the archetypes and not from later adjusted practice. Baptism came at the very beginning of the Christian life, as true 'initiation.' Amongst its many meanings was that it established a basis *of treating people as believers* thereafter. The baptized are believers; and the believers are baptized. If in Acts 10 the Spirit falls upon Gentiles (which had hardly been anticipated), then all that Peter can say is 'Quick! Get the water! We cannot

---

8   It would mean that the scandal of John's baptism lay not in the introduction of a new ritual, but in the application of an existing ritual for cleansing Gentiles to the Jews, the supposedly 'clean,' chosen people.
9   This can lead to special pleading by Baptists! A nice one is that at Corinth the household of Stephanas 'have devoted themselves to the service of the saints' (1 Cor 16.15) and one should 'give recognition to such people' (1 Cor 16.18). *Ergo* the whole household was adult, mature, and articulate! But we have no problem with saying that a family is distinguished, or leading citizens, or even physically energetic, as general characteristics of that family, without for a minute thereby implying that that family has currently no young members or babes in arms!

leave these new believers unbaptized a second longer!' (Acts 10.44–48). The New Testament does not allow for unbaptized believers; all that can be said to them is 'Quick! Get the water!'; and thus delaying the baptism of the children of believers runs the risk (or underlines the policy) of creating a category of unbaptized believers as they grow up.[10]

5. Further confirmation is that all to whom Paul writes his letters are described as baptized. He moves naturally from saying 'you are all children of God through faith in Christ Jesus' (Gal 3.26), to explaining 'for as many of you as have been baptized into Christ have put on Christ' (3.27). He can write that 'all our fathers were under the cloud, all passed through the sea, all were baptized into Moses…but with not all of them was God well pleased…and these things occurred as examples for us…' (1 Cor 10.1–6), and he is virtually saying 'All you Corinthians are baptized…'[11] If this point is taken, then it should be noted that on occasion there are young children present to hear the word read out to them (cf Eph 6.1 and Col 3.20—and in both letters the presumption of baptism in all the hearers has already been made). Children are presumably there from infancy, and Paul's words apply to them whatever their level of understanding. The children are as much members of the baptized community as anyone else, bound by the same moral obligations of discipleship as anyone else, and not separated out from the baptized in any way at all.

6. Lastly, in this cumulative argument, there persists a question from the New Testament: 'How should believers bring up their children?' If the answer is 'As unbelievers to be later converted,' then baptism is certainly inappropriate. But is that the answer? If children in believing homes are being taught to pray to God as 'Father' and to trust in the love of Jesus, who is present with them, then they are in fact being *treated as believers* from the start, and should then be baptized from the start. To treat them in other respects as believers (even in a tentative way) and yet not to baptize them is to fly in the face of the New Testament use of baptism.[12]

---

10 There is a bit of further fun in noting that there is another kind of 'camera-shot' evidence which we do not have. As Paul revisits his old haunts, or writes to them, we nowhere find the children of believing families now reaching the age of credible profession and seeking baptism. Now evidence of *that* sort would have settled the issue…

11 Almost all other citing of Paul's references to baptism show the same pattern—thus, *eg*, in Romans 6, after five chapters of establishing justification through faith, he is ready to see off the objection that his doctrine is a licence to sin by appealing instead to baptism, taking it for granted that all his readers have been baptized.

12 There is a seminal illustration in words attributed to Luther (I have not traced them) that an infant has the faith of a Christian who is asleep. None of us, when asleep, has conscious faith, yet we believe we are still Christians through the night. So could it be that watching an infant from birth to, say, five years of age is (ideally, and within a believing household) watching, not a conversion, but a Christian believer *slowly waking up*? Giving baptism has been entirely appropriate (as with mentally damaged people or those who come to faith near to death, and are semi-conscious when baptized— categories of baptismal candidates where little or no 'waking up' is expected on this earth). A parallel illustration is in footnote 1 on page 27 of my *A Case for Infant Baptism*.

How then do we fit our understanding of infant baptism into the whole picture of baptism? The New Testament provides a great range of baptismal *motifs*: repentance, conversion, adoption, rebirth by the Spirit, being united with Christ in his death and resurrection, becoming a disciple, being put under the headship of Christ (or the name of the Holy Trinity), being transplanted into the body of Christ, walking in newness of life morally, and becoming an inheritor of eternal life and of the final resurrection. It appears reasonable to suggest that everything that is involved in being Christian at all is symbolized in baptism. Thus we go on to say that, whether baptism is given to an infant or an adult, thereafter that baptized person has the same symbolism of the same baptism pertaining to him or her as a baptized person, irrespective of when the baptism was given. And it should be noted that the appeal to baptism in the New Testament is not an appeal to remember one's baptism (as though one could recapture the exact psychological state in which one underwent baptism), but it is an appeal to understand one's baptism and to respond to its meaning—both tasks for the here and now, not dependent upon whether one's memory can 'pick up' the actual experience.[13]

We need to add another feature of the baptismal language of the New Testament—it is performative language. Baptism is treated in the New Testament as actually converting. If today we are used to a split between heart conversion and outward baptism, then we have to be careful in our approach to the New Testament. But if we accept, as I have sought to lay out above, that in principle adults (yes, and households) were converted *in* baptism in the New Testament, then we have the key to understanding the use of the performative language, such as 'Arise and be baptized and wash away your sins' (Acts 22.16).[14] It is not surprising if the language of liturgy from the earliest days has been similarly performative—that is, that baptism is viewed as actually initiating and not simply as reporting an initiation which has actually occurred elsewhere.[15] An applicant comes to baptism unforgiven

---

13 This is true not only to New Testament baptism, but also to the fickleness of human memory, and the inexactness of recall mechanisms! Even a Baptist must acknowledge that amnesia does not wipe out a baptism—he or she remains truly baptized whatever the state of the memory. The important thing is knowing oneself to be a baptized person *here and now*, which is secured by objective evidence, such as a certificate—or photograph.

14 I have chosen this instance simply for the sake of variety. But the performative language (or language of efficacy) is to be found equally in Matt 28.19 (where the natural meaning of the Greek is that we are to make disciples '*by* baptizing…and teaching…'), John 3.5 (where we need not duck the possible instrumentality of the water!), Acts 2.38–39, Rom 6.3–4, 1 Cor 12.13, Gal 3.27, Col 2.11–12, Titus 3.5, 1 Peter 3.18 and elsewhere.

15 This is the passing critique of any Baptist view that baptism is in essence a public and outward witness or testimony to what has already happened inwardly (and therefore somewhat privately) on some previous occasion. It is easy to demonstrate from the New Testament that baptisms might themselves on occasion be somewhat private (as, for example, in the Gaza desert (Acts 8.38), or after midnight and after an earthquake in a Gentile jailer's home in Philippi (Acts 16.33)), however much it may be desirable for them to be public. But the point here is that the key to the nature of baptism must be sought in the sacramental uniting of the outward and inward initiation, not in the making of an oh-so-careful disjunction between them.

and outside of the discipleship of Christ, of the reign of the Holy Trinity, and of the church which is Christ's body. He or she repents of sin, professes the faith, is baptized, and is *thus* incorporated and declared to be now a true member of the body of Christ. The initiation rite initiates.

But does that mean it works automatically or like magic? No, the crucial feature of these initiatory elements is that they come by faith—and without faith baptism is anomalous.[16] And, yes, we are positing faith in the offspring of believers, even as infants, though obviously it is time which will reveal it for sure. Baptism formally unites candidates (adults and infants) to the visible church and formally states that Jesus is Lord to them—but the reality of believing in Jesus as Lord may still not enrich the lives of all who are baptized. In such cases, baptism is still baptism, given once-for-all-for-life. If then faith later dawns in lives of such people, they are not baptized again, but simply rejoice that the inward is now in line with the outward.[17]

Special Question: What of 'Covenant Theology'?

When the Reformers retained infant baptism, they were frequently moved by what has become known as 'covenant theology.' I have to say that it is important, before anyone starts to throw 'covenant theology' into the discussion, that he or she knows precisely what is involved. In the doctrine's most logical form, as maintained by Calvin, this decreed that the covenant of election extended unconditionally to the children of believers, and that 'God pronounces that he adopts our infants as his children before they are born, when he promises that he will be a God to us and to our seed after us. This promise includes their salvation.'[18] This is logical, unmistakeable, powerful—and unsustainable. As Paul King Jewett (a Calvinist Baptist) says 'this noble vision is destined to fade as soon as we lower our eyes from heaven to earth.'[19] The sheer facts of the children of believers belie the doctrine—there cannot be anything automatic or invariable which can make such a doctrine credible, and a practice of infant baptism staked on such a doctrine flies in the face of the facts.

The idea of a 'covenant' with the children of believers nevertheless lives on as a basis for infant baptism. But we need to ask what kind of covenant this is—and the usual answer is that it is a kind of 'external' covenant, which, through believing parents, offers the promises of God to the infant, and conveys 'external' privileges in membership of the visible church and the various means of grace. It makes the inward benefits of the covenant—true

---

16 I choose the word 'anomalous' deliberately—such a baptism is not 'invalid,' but has actually happened. See my chapter on 'What is a Baptism?' in Worship Series no 61 *One Baptism Once* (1978, still in print).

17 See booklet No 61, *One Baptism Once*, throughout.

18 Calvin, *Institutes*, IV, xv, 20.

19 P K Jewett, *Infant Baptism and Confirmation* (Typescript, 1960) p 273.

conversion and rebirth and inheritance of the kingdom of heaven—conditional upon the later (and as yet unknown) response of the recipient of baptism.[20] It rather looks as though the concept of a covenant, which was needed to justify infant baptism because of the place of children in the old covenant, has been salvaged only at great cost to the overall theology of covenant.[21] My own provisional assessment is that even the most avid predestinarians do not help the case for infant baptism by an over-reliance on articulating 'covenant theology.'[22]

That does not mean we cannot join forces. My own 'case' above is that the children of believers are, from the start, properly *treated as* being themselves believers, and are thus, like adults professing the faith, proper candidates for baptism.[23] This is obviously weaker than Calvin's 'covenant' which simply says that they are elect, and it is stronger than the 'external covenant' people who simply say they are admitting the child of believers to certain privileges, and uttering the promises of God over the child and into his or her life. But it is identical with both these covenant theologies in looking for parental faith and discipleship as the key category which qualifies the infant for baptism. The question as to whether and how the *Common Worship* provision suffices to establish the standing of parents for these purposes is handled in chapter 3 below.[24]

---

20 Jewett mocks this as the new covenant which anyone can break, contrary to Jeremiah's prophecy (Jer 31.31–34) of the difference there would be between the old covenant and the new (Jewett, *op cit*, pp 277–9).

21 The 'external' covenant may gain some self-confidence by the famous Pauline phrase, in a passage about marital separation, 'otherwise your children would be unclean, but now they are holy [*or* 'saints']' (1 Cor 7.14). Does this mean they are 'within the covenant'? If it does (and it looks plausible) then the context has the unbelieving marriage partner similarly made holy! And that is difficult enough in itself, before we assert that the unbelieving partner can now be a candidate for baptism *whilst unbelieving*.

22 A short check on modern pedobaptist evangelicals suggests they are generally of the 'external covenant' sort—a typical quote is '[When children show no sign of faith] Baptism has now an evangelistic office...it is a continual pointer to the act they must perform as those within the sphere of the Holy Spirit...' (G W Bromiley, *Children of Promise: The Case for Baptizing Infants* (T & T Clark, 1979) p 81). But authors may vary from one position to another—so Marcel writes (like Calvin) 'By a sovereign decree, independently of any human point of view, God decides that the children of believers shall be included in his covenant' (P Ch Marcel, *The Biblical Doctrine of Infant Baptism* (ET, James Clarke, 1953) p 191). But even he is ready to go on and say there are 'children of believers who refuse to confirm the covenant' (*op cit*, p 208), and thus, despite his very strong earlier language, the 'covenant' was, under analysis, a gospel offer, but not an actual bonding by regeneration by the Spirit.

23 I have ventured elsewhere to distinguish methodologies in a way which I hope is helpful—the 'covenant theology' people (of either camp) wish to establish a general principle of the covenant, and read off from it, deductively, what the implications are for children of believers (and in fact happily conclude such children can be baptized); whereas I (distrusting both camps in part) want to examine the evidence of the use of baptism in the New Testament (without precluding straws in the wind from the Old) and then, by an inductive procedure, to set out, however provisionally, as consistent a doctrine of the relationship of households, baptism, gospel and church membership as that procedure warrants (see my *Infant Baptism and the Gospel* (DLT, 1973) pp 16–17).

24 See especially pp 18–20. It is at this point also that I commend the pressure group Baptismal Integrity (previously MORIB), of which I am President, as seeking to highlight this doctrinal principle.

3
Liturgical Principles in Baptism

So we come to the Church of England liturgies for baptism, and particularly to the *Common Worship* rite for infant baptism. We start with some tabulated historical background, all of which illuminates the new rite.

The BCP Rites

Cranmer provided in 1549 and 1552 an infant rite only, refined in two stages from the pre-Reformation rites, and intended for the whole nation at the point of each child's birth. His process has often been criticized as dealing with a rite for infants as though it had a kind of autonomous life of its own, but in fact on inspection it proves that he handles his revision largely on general principles of baptism, which must have been well formed in his mind, even if he never in his own lifetime conducted or witnessed the baptism of an adult.[25] Thus we find:

a) A formal theological structure in which one born as a child of Adam and with the entail of original sin comes to express repentance and faith, to be baptized, and to be declared regenerate;

b) As formal variants from a rite for adults:

   i)   No statement that the candidate has committed actual sin;

   ii) The use of the Mark 10.13–16 gospel passage already noted;

   iii) Addressing of questions intended for the candidate to the persons of the godparents with the requirement that they answer 'in the name of this child';

   iv) A 'fall-back' provision in relation to the 'dipping' of the candidate (which is the norm)—if the godparents certify that the child is weak '*it shall suffice to pour water upon it.*'

We need not stay on the elements he changed or eliminated, which were partly structural but more especially ceremonial.[26] They also included the presupposition that the unbaptized child had an unclean spirit and needed to be exorcized, and this he mercifully removed.

The main formal problems (apart from that gospel reading) which his rite left for future generations were as follows:

---

25 The main positive evidence for this statement is the ease with which the rite for 'those of Riper Years' was adapted from his rite for infants in 1661–2. The main complaint one would make of his rite is the wretched use of Mark 10 as the Gospel reading, and the totally lame attempt to justify infant baptism from that reading in the liturgical homily which follows.

26 In the Sarum and 1549 rites the water was 'consecrated' quite apart from the actual liturgy and kept in the font ready for use, and the rite itself had its first part at the church door prior to admission within the building for the baptism to occur at the font.

a) The profession of faith is detached a long way from the actual baptism, largely through the introduction of a prayer over the water following the responses in 1552;
b) The request 'Name this child' has always looked (and been believed) as though the child received its name for the first time at that point in its life;[27]
c) The mandatory signing with the sign of the cross after baptism not only irritated the Puritans (by making requisite that which Scripture did not), but also it came with the performative phrase 'We receive this child into the congregation of Christ's flock,' which appeared to make both the words and action ('...and do sign *him* with the sign of the cross') far more important than was warranted.

In 1662, three further minor changes rather exacerbated the problems:
a) A third question and answer was added to the vows of repentance and faith:

> Wilt thou then obediently keep God's holy will and commandments and walk in the same all the days of thy life?
> **I will.**

b) A 'consecration' of the baptismal water was added back into the prayer over the water;[28]
c) When a child was baptized privately in a home (because in danger of death) but afterwards lived and was brought to church, then the post-baptismal 'reception into the church' and signing with the cross were done at that point, even more strongly (and wrongly) suggesting that 'reception into the church' was an event separable from baptism and subsequent to it.

It has to be added that the resultant 1662 rite for infant baptism is incredibly heavy and tortuous in its language, and extremely hard going for those not often in church, and all the more as coming after the second lection at Morning or Evening Prayer making it all the heavier in practice.[29] Even the Prayer Book Society itself is never heard urging its use today, and no-one in the Liturgical Publishing Group or the General Synod ever seems to have wanted to provide the ancient text to stand alongside the modern in the *Common*

---

27 In 1549 the child's name was used prior to the point of baptism, though it did look as though it was conferred at that point, but in 1552 that earlier use ceased. Furthermore Cranmer himself wrote into the catechism the misleading question and answer:
    Who gave you this name?
    My godfathers and godmothers *in my baptism*. (Italics COB's)
28 'Sanctify this water to the mystical washing away of sin.'
29 It was never intended (or rubrically permitted) as a 'stand alone' service, though from the nineteenth century onwards the '4 o'clock' use of it in new urban parishes of close-packed humanity obscured this fact.

Worship books, as was done with other services.[30]

Did the Puritans ever object to 'Seeing...that this child is regenerate'? The answer appears to be 'Not during the first hundred years, but, yes, at the Savoy Conference in 1661, when, because of the pressures of the Caroline bishops, the response of the understandably paranoid puritans was to tooth-comb their way through the pre-Commonwealth Prayer Book and object to everything they possibly could.' On the whole the formal structure and per-formative theological language of a biblical baptismal rite seem to have been properly understood in the context of a reformed theology.[31] The days of a real controversy on the issue lay ahead in the nineteenth century.[32]

Series 1,2,3 and ASB

Modern baptismal rites in the Church of England have a kind of family connection. We leave aside 'Series 1' which was in 1966 the legalization of the 1928 rite, itself a slightly streamlined version of 1662.[33] The new 'family' began with trial or 'study' rites in 1959. These took an adult baptism-plus-confirmation-plus-communion as the 'archetype,' and derived their infant rite, not unfairly, from it. The following elements from 1959 are still found in *Common Worship* in one way or another:

a) infant baptism as a 'stand alone' (main—not 4 o'clock) service (though it could be within other services), and thus including a ministry of the word (and no Mark 10.13–16!);

b) a proper recognition in the rite that parents have a prior role before god-parents in presenting their own children for baptism, and in accepting the responsibilities of bringing them up—and an opening exhortation which includes their 'example' in relation to 'public worship';

---

30 Perhaps someone could tell us which rite was chosen by the Prince of Wales when his sons were baptized in the early 1980s—and on what grounds it was chosen!

31 I use the words 'formal structure' both to indicate that an initiation rite will properly have an actual initiation into Christ built into its text, and also to underline a point which often escapes those who do not like the language of regeneration in baptism—that is, that you have to dismember the whole rite line by line to evacuate the concept, and it cannot be achieved by merely fudging one line.

32 In 1846–7 the then Bishop of Exeter, Henry Philpotts, charged George Gorham, who had been nominated to an incumbency in his diocese, with heresy. Gorham denied that all infants were necessarily and invariably regenerated in baptism, and that was viewed by the Bishop as sufficient grounds to decline to institute him. Gorham brought a case in the (Canterbury provincial) Court of Arches, seeking an injunction requiring the Bishop to institute him. Philpotts defended himself on the grounds of the alleged heresy, and the Court found for the Bishop in 1849. Gorham appealed to the Judicial Committee of the Privy Council, who reversed the decision in March 1850, stating that Gorham's doctrine was compatible with the Anglican formularies, and thus giving an authoritative basis to the belief that affirmations of regeneration in baptism are conditional. The reversal was in part due to the magisterial work of scholarship of William Goode, *The Effects of Infant Baptism* (1849), a book which showed that virtually all Anglican theologians from the sixteenth century to the early nineteenth had held a position comparable to Gorham's, and that Philpotts' doctrine was itself relatively newly adopted. The whole controversy is well written up in J C S Nias, *Gorham and the Bishop of Exeter* (Church Historical Society/SPCK, 1951).

33 Its licence was regularly renewed as an 'alternative service' until 1980, when it was allowed to lapse.

13

c) a profession of faith (for infants not the full Apostles' Creed) last thing before the actual baptism;

d) an allocating of baptismal imagery to a weighty 'blessing of the font';

e) an elimination of 'reception into the church,' whereby only baptism itself appears as 'performative';

f) the innovation of an (optional) post-baptismal giving of a candle.

These rites lurked in the offing till the Liturgical Commission addressed 'Series 2' in 1966–67, when 'alternative services' could for the first time be authorized for use. Series 2 services so revised 1959 that the infant rite moved on as follows:

a) The opening exhortation became a rubrical injunction;

b) The readings of Scripture became two short pastiches;[34]

c) A new and far-reaching structural change divided the 'repentance' from the 'faith'—so that the former, cross-headed 'The Decision,' came at, say, the front of the congregation, and the latter, bracketed with the actual administration of the water under the cross-heading 'The Baptism,' followed the 'Blessing of the Water' at the font (which in many buildings meant a long procession);[35]

d) The overtly proxy form of the vows in 1959 was superseded by a deliberately ambiguous form of introduction to the vows, obviously addressed to parents and sponsors:

  i) At the Decision: 'Those who bring children to be baptized must affirm their allegiance to Christ and their rejection of all that is evil.'

  ii) At the profession of faith: 'You must now make the Christian profession in which they [these children] are to be baptized, and in which you will bring them up.'

  In each case, whilst the formal point that the vows are those of the candidate *could* be made, the wording had a strong leaning in popular understanding towards the opposite view, that in fact the parents and sponsors were being interrogated about themselves—and, of course, for all sorts of pastoral reasons, such a view was very welcome in many circles.

e) After the post-baptismal ceremonies (the sign of the cross and the optional candle) there came for the first time a 'welcome.'[36]

The bones of much of our present rite were beginning to appear, and the simplicity of language and structure commended the rite strongly.

---

34 Mark 10 made a brief reappearance in the second of these!

35 Although the first set of questions at 'The Decision' took up the 'repentance' theme, an urge towards 'being positive' led the Commission to make the first question 'Do you turn to Christ?' (which was apparently widely welcomed).

36 It was not given a separate cross-heading, and it was optional, but it made an important theological point with its opening: 'God has received you by baptism into his Church. We therefore welcome you...'

14

Series 3 rite came over ten years after Series 2, and, after a short separate life of its own, it was adapted into conformity with other services of the ASB, and became part of it in November 1980. It was in modern English, and had an interesting new departure. For the first time in a thousand years, the Church of England had a *household* rite—one for adults, infants and children together—as its 'archetype' or norm. True missionary baptism is household baptism (see the New Testament—QED); and one baptism which is common to adults and infants is best held together with a common theology if a household baptism is constructed as its prime liturgical expression, and separate rites are then 'read off' from the primary one.

There were some other new touches in the rite:

a) The opening rubrics of 1959 and Series 2, were now turned into a statement of the need of parental 'example,' followed by the question as to whether the parents and godparents would give it—and their response 'I am willing.'

b) The Decision, first demarcated in Series 2, now had both the sign of the cross brought to enrich it and also a prayer for protection ('May almighty God deliver you from the powers of darkness...') added to it.[37] Thus all the treatment of evil was neatly and forcefully grouped into the Decision.

c) The profession of faith was topped up by a congregational affirmation:
This is the faith of the Church.
This is our faith.
We believe and trust...

d) Both sets of vows were introduced by a formula which outdated the ambiguity of Series 2—in each case the parents and godparents were told 'You must answer for yourselves and for these children.'

e) The Welcome now became a separate and mandatory section, and, in the context of Communion, led naturally into the Peace.[38]

f) An opening note provided for the possibility of anointing with oil at the time of signing with the sign of the cross.[39]

---

37 The signing with the sign of the cross was still allowed to come after baptism, but here in The Decision was clearly the preferred position.

38 This is worth noting, as, when Series 2 was first authorized in February 1968, the sharing of the Peace at any Communion service was still a rare occurrence, and was just being learned from the introduction five months earlier of Series 2 Communion.

39 This optional provision was forced in at Revision Stage in Synod by people who threatened to vote against the whole service if they did not get it, and so it came in without text, without theology, and without rationale. It is indeed arguable that, if it has meaning, it means something different when the signing comes before baptism from what it means when it comes after. Here in Southwark diocese we used to have an exposition of the 'before' meaning in the Maundy Thursday rite at the cathedral, whilst the diocesan printed rite for adult baptism-and-confirmation provided an 'after' position for the actual signing. Few made the disconnection...

Another feature of the Series 3 and ASB rites was the provision of services of 'Thanksgiving after Childbirth' and 'Thanksgiving after Adoption,' services helping with the range of adaptable post-natal rites (and also giving a final resting-place to Mark 10.13–16, all reference to which had now been removed from the Scripture pastiche in the infant baptism rite).

Common Worship Infant Baptism
A) Its Continuity By Descent
It is against the ASB background that the *Common Worship* rites have come into use. The following features set out above run on into the new infant baptism service:
1. Adult and infant rites have a common theology, secured by household baptism as a liturgical norm.
2. The language of the rite is 'categorical' or 'performative.'
3. The structure of the 'The Liturgy of Baptism' still follows the same basic pattern (with brief additions), as is set out on pages 346 and 348 of the *CW* main Book:
   Presentation of the Candidates (if not done before The Liturgy of the Word)
   The Decision
   Signing with the Cross
   Prayer over the Water
   Profession of Faith
   Baptism
   Commission
   [Prayers of Intercession]
   The Welcome and Peace
The pattern has gained a clear 'Presentation' and 'Commission' (and the optional Prayers), and, interestingly, has lost the 'Giving of a Lighted Candle,' which has been attached at the end to 'The Sending Out.'
It should be clear that there is real family continuity in this, as well as one or two unexpected features of a new generation. It is worth looking at some general features of the new baptismal rites, and then at some specifically 'infant' questions.

B) Some General Liturgical Features
a) *The Presentation* (p 352). The manner of 'presentation' is not prescribed, but the implication is that some naming of the candidates to the congregation by those presenting them should begin the baptismal section.[40]

---

40 As noted above, the Structure pages on baptism allow the Presentation to come earlier in the service, before the Collect, if desired; but this is the barest permission, which has no comparable rubric at that point in the full text.

b) *The Decision* (p 353). The Decision appears in continuity with its predecessor in the ASB—but the profession of faith which follows at the baptism itself (p 356), now in the form of the Apostles' Creed, is the central affirmation of faith in the rite. So the questions at the Decision have no need as before to cover the doctrine of the Trinity, and are best understood as, in the first three, expanding the second and third questions from the ASB, and, in the second three, expanding the first question in the ASB (which had been in an odd order which is now corrected[41]). A rubric, added in 2000, permits the ASB form, which is printed on page 372, and can be used if there are '*strong pastoral reasons.*'[42]

c) *The Prayer over the Water* (p 355). It remains policy to put biblical imagery, history and theology into this prayer, which makes it weighty. There are, for the first time, alternative texts—a responsive form of the prayer (p 364) and three different 'high seasonal' texts (pp 365–9). Despite the linguistic weight, the 'sanctifying' of the water (or rather of its use) is a much less defined theological concept than the 'consecration' of eucharistic elements. Emergency baptism can do without such a prayer;[43] if baptism is done in a swimming pool or river, no-one worries as to the extent of water covered by the prayer;[44] and few can mind too much about the destination of the water after baptism—all over a floor or soaking into a carpet or being rubbed off a candidate onto a towel!

d) *The Profession of Faith* (p 356). The Apostles' Creed is back, some 30 years after it was set aside. It is in question-and-answer form, and the questions retain the emphatic 'believe and trust' which has come to be viewed as including commitment as well as cerebral affirmation. The difference is that the whole congregation recites it, though the candidates are picked out in the opening words of the officiant. Once again, as with the Decision, those '*strong pastoral reasons*' may be indulged by the use of the ASB form, which, marginally re-touched, appears on page 373.

e) *The Baptism* (p 357). As in all Church of England rites, the mode of baptism is, in the first instance, 'dipping' and, as a fall-back, 'pouring.' There is no provision for sprinkling or smearing, which ought only to be contemplated with candidates in intensive care (the full notes say '*water must*

---

41 See the account of compiling the Series 2 texts (1968) on page 14 above.
42 What on earth would count as such '*strong pastoral reasons*'? The honest answer seems to be something like 'when the officiant doesn't like the new form,' though other reasons may be imaginable. Personally I regret this retrogressive fall-back. One grumble I have heard about the new is a dislike of reference to the devil—but it is in the baptismal liturgies that our Church has most consistently acknowledged his continued existence, as fighting against the devil has gone with the signing with the cross throughout, even when the renunciations have not mentioned him.
43 See *Pastoral Services*, page 195.
44 Or, with a flowing river (as desired in, say, the Didache), should one pray over the water a calculated distance upstream from the candidates…?

at least flow on the skin of the candidate'[45]). The full notes also strongly urge the threefold use of the water with the threefold naming of the persons of the Trinity.[46] And, whilst the submersion of an infant may require some dexterity, those requesting the baptism should be allowed a clear choice between the two modes, just as in the case of adults.

f) *The Post-baptismal Ceremonies* (pp 357 and 363). For the sake of completeness, we note the following further options: (i) a clothing (perhaps for those who have been submerged); (ii) the signing with the cross (if not used earlier); and (iii) the new idea of giving a candle at the very end of the service.[47]

C) Specifically 'Infant' Features

This is the point to separate out and put together those features of the CW baptism rite which are to the fore when infants are to be baptized:

a) *The questioning of parents.* Those who believe (in line with the biblical evidence in chapter 2 above) that it is the Christian standing of parents which qualifies infants for baptism inevitably want a properly Christian profession to be made by the parents. In part this must be covered in preparation (see the Canons and notes on them in Appendix 3 below); but it is formally expressed also in the service. The crucial questions to the parents and godparents are on page 352. They are not now wrapped together with the candidates' vows in the Decision, but stand alone. Whilst they may not have the stark character of 'You must answer for yourselves as well as these infants,' they are nevertheless equally searching in realistic terms. They are further reinforced by the requirement that the parents and godparents join in the responsive form of the creed (page 356), and by the placing of responsibility upon them in the Commission (page 358). All these elements of the liturgy also assist those preparing parents for the baptism of their infants.

b) *The proxy vows of infants.* 'The Decision' has six questions, and they are now clearly addressed to the candidates alone, whether adults or infants, for the rubric says that infants are themselves being questioned *'through their parents and godparents.'* Thus this section is not of itself intended to clarify the standing or faith of the sponsors, who have already been questioned as shown under (a) above. These vows belong to the candidates, expressing the baptismal obligations which are to bind those who are being baptized, obligations exactly the same as those for adults, part of

---

45 The 'full notes' are not printed on page 344, but reference is made there to the set in the 1998 *Common Worship: Initiation Services*—and this is from Note 12 on page 18 there.
46 See the same Note 12.
47 The connection there is made with the candle lit at the time of The Decision, and it is possible to include candle-bearing neophytes and/or parents of the newly baptized into a procession as a kind of triumphal statement. It also means that 'when to put the candle out' is a less pressing question...

the holding together of adult and infant baptism.[48] In short, there are two kinds of responses which the ASB had united in one, but *Common Worship* has properly separated out. The mere separation does not imply any loss of the force of either.

c) *Admission to communion.* It is relatively commonplace nowadays to note that baptism in principle admits to communion. However, the Church of England is still moving towards a not-quite-regular policy of admission to communion at around the age of seven, so that the baptism rite cannot easily sound as though it is opening the door to the Lord's table.[49]

d) *The Commission.* This has only a rubric in the folding cards, but is set out in full in the main book on page 358. The basic idea of The Commission, as addressed to candidates able to answer for themselves (on which see page 359), is that living the baptismal life should, logically and in the economy of God's grace, spring *from* baptism, and is best set out liturgically *after* it. At infant baptism, it comes to reinforce the responsible role of parents and others in the Christian upbringing of the children.

e) *Going on—including issues of unrepeatability.* A booklet of this size can do little more than simply expound the rite. But it is important to remind ourselves that even an infant baptism has, at root, the same awesome meaning as the baptism of an adult Jew or Muslim. And, once given, it is given for life. A baptized person is a baptized person for the rest of his or her life. Whatever else can be given (such as a renewal of baptismal vows), the one thing that cannot be given is a baptism pure and simple. Our difficulty is that, even within the life of the church, many parts of the Church of England, having given infant baptism, do not handle it as a resource in people's lives thereafter, but let it drop in embarrassment.[50]

---

48 In other words, the oddity is not that proxy vows are expressed, but that it would be odd if there were one kind of baptism (adult) with obligations to walk in newness of life expressed, and another (infant) in which no obligations attached to the lives of the candidates at all. It would be even more shriekingly anomalous when at confirmation, as it is currently conducted, the candidates were asked to ratify and acknowledge for themselves that they were bound by those baptismal promises, when, on this hypothesis, they had no baptismal vows or obligations with which to engage at all.

49 Quite the reverse—we still have the shrieking anomaly that the newly baptized are (at The Welcome) 'all baptized into one body,' but, if the baptism is conducted at a Communion service, then five minutes later the president and congregation may well be saying:
   We who are many are one body,
   for we all share in the one bread.
And this is to excorporate the newly incorporated baptized infants who are in fact non-communicant. Order One does, however, allow other words at the breaking of the bread, and they may be less embarrassing! I refer readers back to 1 Cor 10 (quoted on page 7 above) where the baptized and the communicant were co-extensive, and the baptized non-communicant was unimaginable. For a fuller treatment, see Peter Reiss, *Children in Communion* (Grove Worship booklet W 149, 1997), where the House of Bishops' Guidelines are set out also.

50 For further handling of these themes, I refer readers back to my, still in print, *One Baptism Once* (Grove Booklet on Ministry and Worship No 61, 1978), which includes a chapter on 'Preaching to the Baptized.' For a (dramatic) renewal of baptismal vows in water, see my, *Renewal of Baptismal Vows* (Grove Worship booklet W 124, 1993).

4

Implementing the New Rite

Finally, I add a few practical tips for staging the *Common Worship* infant baptism rite, to be used, of course, in the context of the main service of Sunday.[51]

There ought to be a 'Preparation' and 'Liturgy of the Word.' The Preparation can include a 'Thanksgiving Prayer for a Child.'[52] The 'Presentation' may also come after the Introduction (see the Structure on pp 346 and 348) and there are various creative ways in which parents and godparents may 'present' their candidate by name to the officiant and congregation (and this may also be assisted by information in a news-sheet or other handout). It will be a matter of local decision as to whether it is better to do this early in the service, or leave it to be part of the 'Liturgy of Baptism' proper.

When the baptism section begins, it is appropriate for the Presentation and the Decision to be taken in a front row, or with the baptismal parties turning to face the congregation from the front, or even to have officiant and respondents facing each other in front of the congregation and at 90 degrees to them. The officiant should be in position to address the congregation at the right point (see p 352), and may even want the people to stand for that response. It is worth a dramatic pause for the lighting of the candle before the Decision, and the sense of passing from darkness to light needs to be reinforced by it. If it simply holds up the action, or seems irrelevant, it is better not done.

For the Signing with the Cross, it is helpful if all those being signed are facing the congregation—that is, babes being very visible in front of the people. The officiant can then sign each (and invite parents and godparents to do so also), go to one side and face the congregation, and trigger a strong congregational exhortation when each has been signed. He or she can then stretch out an arm towards the candidates for the 'apotropaic' prayer.

The next stages depend on where the baptismal font is placed. If it is at the West end, then a procession (perhaps with singing) may be the way to get there. If the congregation are at all likely to be remote from the baptism, then they may well be encouraged to gather round outside of the baptismal parties during the singing—perhaps with small children sitting on the floor very near the font. Proximity and visibility are the key to participation.[53] It works well to have the baptismal water (preferably slightly warmed) in a

---

51 See Canon B21 on page 23 below—but I know it is difficult in some places.
52 A Thanksgiving Prayer came in Appendix 1 to the 1998 *Initiation Services* (on p 72), and is simply included in the 'Supplementary Texts' cited in the Notes on p 344; the Prayer is distinct from any in the separate service of Thanksgiving for the Gift of a Child.

large jug or ewer and to pour it visibly and audibly into the font when the Prayer over the Water is to begin. Then comes the Profession of Faith, which should, through proximity, have the congregation carrying the parents and godparents into bold affirmation. Then comes the baptism—by dipping or pouring, and desirably in a threefold mode.[54] How to hold an infant and discourage yelling is beyond the brief of this booklet, but a child lying back so that even a good dose of water applied to the forehead runs off the top of the head is a good recipe (and even so, the family should have a towel handy).

If the font is in fact near the front of the congregation from the beginning of the service, it may still be worth asking them to gather round—but, facing this way, once they have stood for the Prayer over the Water and the Profession of Faith, they can then sit for the actual baptism, and see it easily.

After the baptism, whilst there may be optional ceremonies, the main provision is one prayer, a return from the font (for which again singing may be appropriate), and the Commission, which, when infants are being baptized, may conclude with a prayer. Then come the Intercessions, though there is an awkwardness in taking the focus away from the baptism to the needs of the world, and then coming back to the candidates for the Welcome and Peace which follow.[55] The Welcome is best done with the congregation seated, and may involve officiant or family persons carrying newly baptized infants down a centre aisle and up again, and turning to face the congregation for a round of applause (the rubric says 'The congregation may greet the newly baptized'). Then the congregation are invited to stand for the Peace.

The last distinctive feature of this baptismal liturgy is the Giving of a Lighted Candle. Once again the infants are addressed in the second person, but through their parents and godparents (who are actually going to receive and carry the candles). If there is a hymn following the blessing (a not unusual practice), then the candles may be lit and presented during the hymn. Then, at its conclusion, those holding the candles can be asked to hold them high, so that all can see them, whilst the officiant's text and the congregation's response highlight the theme of light, and the Dismissal is also written to embody the theme of light. In many churches the baptismal parties will march out in the procession, ideally still holding their candles high.

The parish baptismal register should be kept scrupulously accurately, and a proper certificate of baptism given by the parish to the newly baptized.

---

53 Merely turning the congregation round in their existing rows can be self-defeating, for it is then impossible to sit, so the baptism is likely to be invisible to the large proportion of them.

54 If by any chance it is submersion which is being used, then quite a bit of the advice here will need to be adapted—though infants can be submerged in relatively small bowls or portable baths, and the issue of submersion should not be made to hang on the provision of a full-blown built-in tank!

55 This problem has always been built into the 'eucharistic' shape, and was solved in previous rites simply by eliminating the intercessions, so that the baptismal material led naturally into the Welcome. If, of course, there is no Communion, then intercessions may come later—and even if there is Communion, the intercessions may still be dropped, as in the previous rites.

Appendix 1
Thanksgiving for the Gift of a Child

The Thanksgiving for the Gift of a Child, which comes in the main *Common Worship* book and also in *Pastoral Services* and is available in folding card form, is strictly not a concern of this Grove booklet. But the availability of such a service does in many parishes enable some sorting out to be done as between parents who truly want their children brought up within the life of Christ and of his church, and those who really only want to go church once, and do not expect to make any commitment to their Lord. The Thanksgiving rite is designed to allow people in good conscience to say 'Thank you' to God the once; and then go on their way without vows or obligations binding upon either themselves or their children. In some parishes it precedes baptism; in some it is offered as an honest alternative to it. But, whilst it is a perinatal rite, it is most distinctly not baptism, and it is a little beyond the scope of this booklet to offer policies in relation to it.[56]

Appendix 2
Emergency Baptism

Emergency baptism is to be found in *Pastoral Services*, page 195. The Notes on page 198 provide that if necessary a lay person may administer the baptism, and the text on page 195 indicates that a 'Prayer over the Water' is not necessary (whilst even a lay person may (unsurprisingly) say a blessing). The Notes also make clear that such a baptism should not really arise from superstition (though a time of danger of death is no time to debate theology), and that the name of the child does not have to have been decided—the crucial matter is identification (so the text might be something like 'Newborn son of Mrs Sarah Jones, I baptize you in the name...'). Such baptisms should be properly registered, and there is provision on page 198 for the later Welcome in the congregation, if the child recovers.

---

56 Grove Worship booklet W 165 (August 2001) is planned to be *Common Worship Thanksgiving for the Gift of a Child* by Trevor Lloyd, and deals with parish policy issues.

The Canons of the Church of England

B21 Of Holy Baptism
It is desirable that every minister having a cure of souls shall normally administer the sacrament of Holy Baptism on Sundays at public worship when the most number of people come together, that the congregation there present may witness the receiving of them that be newly baptized into Christ's Church, and be put in remembrance of their own profession made to God in their baptism.

B22 Of the baptism of infants
1. Due notice, normally of at least a week, shall be given before a child is brought to the church to be baptized.
2. If a minister shall refuse or unduly delay to baptize any such infant, the parents or guardians may apply to the bishop of the diocese, who shall, after consultation with the minister, give such directions as he thinks fit.
3. The minister shall instruct the parents or guardians of an infant to be admitted to Holy Baptism that the same responsibilities rest on them as are in the service of Holy Baptism required of the godparents.
4. No minister shall refuse or, save for the purpose of preparing or instructing the parents or guardians or godparents, delay to baptize any infant within his cure that is brought to the church to be baptized, providing that due notice has been given and the provisions relating to the godparents in these Canons are observed.
5. A minister who intends to baptize any infant whose parents are residing outside the boundaries of his cure, unless the names of such persons or one of them be on the church electoral roll of the same, shall not proceed to the baptism without having sought the good will of the minister of the parish in which the parents reside.
[Paragraphs 6, 7, 8, 9 relate to emergency baptism.]

B23 Of godparents and sponsors
1. For every child to be baptized there shall be not fewer than three godparents, of whom at least two shall be of the same sex as the child and of whom at least one shall be of the opposite sex; save that, when three godparents cannot conveniently be had, one godfather and godmother shall suffice. Parents may be godparents for their own children provided that the child have one other godparent.

2. The godparents shall be persons who will faithfully fulfil their responsibilities both by their care of children committed to their charge and by the example of their own godly living.
3. When one who is of riper years is to be baptized he shall choose three, or at least two, to be his sponsors, who shall be ready to present him at the font and afterwards put him in mind of his Christian profession and duties.
4. No person shall be admitted to be a sponsor or godparent who has not been baptized and confirmed. Nevertheless the minister shall have power to dispense with the requirement of confirmation in any case in which in his judgment need so requires.

Notes on the Canons

The background in the 1604 Canons is the expectation that the whole country would be Christian and Anglican! The modifying of them in the 1960s has produced an odd-looking result, but the bones of a missionary concern are there. Godparents are to be of 'godly living' (B23(2)) and to be 'baptized and confirmed' (an exception at the minister's discretion being godly non-Anglicans) (B23(4)). Parents or guardians are to recognize that the same responsibilities rest on them (B22(3)). Whilst, with believing parents, the baptism should go ahead gladly, yet often there may understandably be need for 'preparation' (B22(4)), and that justifies 'delay' (B22(2) and(4)). It is ambiguous as to what is 'preparation'—a minimalist notion being that a visit by a minister, or attendance at an instruction session by a parent, would be 'preparation.' A rounder view would see preparation as providing an actual and tested Christian conviction in the parents, attested by their having become worshippers so that they can genuinely respond that they will 'draw' the children by their 'example into the community of faith' (page 352). We would not count 'preparation' for exams *as* preparation unless there were strong evidence that what we were communicating *had actually gone in*!

There is a grievance procedure (B22(2)). Parents who think themselves 'unduly' delayed may apply to the bishop. He consults the minister, and gives a ruling, which is final. There is no appeal to statute law, as there is no 'right' to baptism in statute law. The bishop represents the final point in a wholly churchly decision about the infant candidate.